Devon

Michael Bennie

COUNTRYSIDE BOOKS
NEWBURY BERKSHIRE

First Published 2007
© Michael Bennie, 2007

COUNTRYSIDE BOOKS
3 Catherine Road
Newbury, Berkshire

To view our complete range of books,
please visit us at
www.countrysidebooks.co.uk

ISBN 978 1 84674 016 9

*Cover picture of the River Avon at Bantham
supplied by Derek Forss*

Photographs by the author
Maps by Gelder Design & Mapping

Designed by Peter Davies, Nautilus Design

Produced through MRM Associates Ltd, Reading
Typeset by CJWT Solutions, St Helens
Printed by Cambridge University Press

Contents

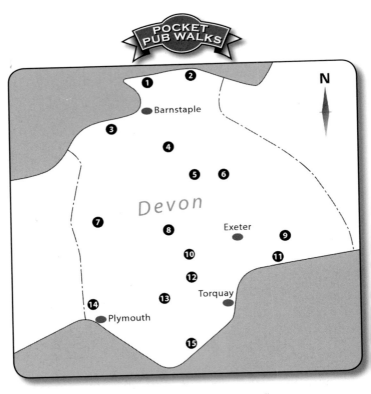

POCKET PUB WALKS

N

① ②

● Barnstaple

③

④

⑤ ⑥

Devon

⑦ ⑧ Exeter ⑨

⑩ ⑪

⑫

⑬ Torquay

⑭ ● Plymouth

⑮

Area map showing location of the walks

Introduction

This varied collection of circuits covers the wide range of walking experiences that Devon has to offer. You will find coastal walks, moorland walks, woodland walks, riverside walks and farmland walks. The routes take you past historic houses, industrial remains, sites of particular natural beauty and pretty, unspoilt villages. I have chosen them for their interest and visual appeal, trying at the same time to illustrate the rich variety of scenery to be found in this most attractive of counties.

We are extremely lucky in Devon. There are over 3,000 miles of public footpaths across the county – and that does not take account of the large areas of access land on Dartmoor and the areas of open land recently opened up to walkers as a result of the Countryside and Rights of Way Act. Moreover, signposting is usually good, and landowners are generally friendly and welcoming, provided, of course, that walkers respect the countryside and the rights of those who live there.

One of the attractions of walking in this area is discovering somewhere to refresh oneself after one's efforts and reflect on the walk; so each route starts and finishes at an attractive pub – either old favourites of mine or new discoveries that have caught my attention. Of course, any selection of this kind is bound to be subjective, and both the choice and the descriptions are based on my own preferences and impressions. But you will find a wide variety of hostelries: some are very old, others are relatively modern; some have particularly interesting histories, others have been chosen for their atmosphere. Something they all have in common, though, is that they offer a warm welcome to visitors.

In addition to the pub and route descriptions, there is information on where to park. Usually pub licensees have no objection to customers leaving their cars in their car parks while they are walking, but occasionally the pub car park is too small (or there isn't one). If you do use the pub car park, it is only polite to ask permission first. There is a sketch map for each walk, numbered to correspond to the numbered paragraphs in the route descriptions, but for added interest, I would recommend that you also carry the relevant OS Explorer map for the area.

None of the walks covers particularly rough or boggy ground, and some can easily be done in trainers. In sections of some of the routes, however, the going can be wet or muddy at times and so I would recommend stout shoes or boots, which will be able to cope with any conditions you are likely to encounter.

Finally, I would like to thank my walking companions, Rod and Jill Latham, Keith Walter and Simon McCandlish, whose company and conversation have, as ever, enlivened my researches.

Michael Bennie

Publisher's Note

We hope that you obtain considerable enjoyment from this book; great care has been taken in its preparation. However, changes of landlord and actual closures are sadly not uncommon. Likewise, although at the time of publication all routes followed public rights of way or permitted paths, diversion orders can be made and permissions withdrawn.

We cannot, of course, be held responsible for such diversion orders and any inaccuracies in the text which result from these or any other changes to the routes nor any damage which might result from walkers trespassing on private property. We are anxious, though, that all details covering the walks and the pubs are kept up to date and would therefore welcome information from readers which would be relevant to future editions.

The simple sketch maps that accompany the walks in the book are based on notes made by the author whilst checking out the routes on the ground. For the benefit of a proper map, however, we do recommend that you purchase the relevant Ordnance Survey sheet covering your walk. The Ordnance Survey maps are widely available, especially through booksellers and local newsagents.

1 Lee

The Grampus Inn

Lee is a pretty little village, set among some spectacular scenery. The coast here is particularly dramatic, and it is hardly surprising that it was known in the past as the haunt of smugglers and wreckers – indeed, Lee was the home of one of the most notorious, Hannibal Richards. The walk takes you along the coast, where you can appreciate the superb views. It then follows farm paths and tracks inland, with more views, before going down the beautiful, densely wooded Borough Valley to return to Lee.

Devon

Distance – 4¼ miles.

OS Explorer 139 Bideford, Ilfracombe and Barnstaple.
GR 484464.
A steep climb to start, and some steps down a steep hill
midway, but otherwise fairly level, with clear paths, tracks
and lanes.

Starting point The Grampus Inn. By prior arrangement
(either by phone in advance or in person on the day),
customers may park in the pub car park while walking.
There is also a public car park at the top of the village.

How to get there *The village is just west of the A361
Ilfracombe to Barnstaple road. It is signed from the Ilfracombe
direction. If you are coming from Barnstaple, turn left onto the
B3343 Woolacombe road and then follow the signs for Lee.*

THE PUB The **Grampus** was originally a farmhouse, but became a
pub in 1975. It is full of character, with low beams and small
windows. The thick, stone walls are colour-washed on the
outside but bare inside. The public area comprises a bar with
a large fireplace (which now houses a wood-burning stove)
and a small family room. There is also a colourful, flower-filled
garden behind. The food ranges from baguettes and ploughman's
lunches to a variety of daily specials, using local produce where
possible.

*Open from 11.30 am to 11 pm or later. As the landlord says,
however, they tend to keep Devon time, which could mean
closing for an hour or so during the day if things are quiet; so
it is probably best to check in advance.*
☎ *01271 862906*

Turn right from the pub. At the T-junction in a few yards, turn sharp left. After 100 yards turn right up **Home Lane**. The lane climbs steeply out of the village to a T-junction; turn right here. Continue to climb. Towards the top, look right for a magnificent view across **Lee** to the woods along **Borough Valley**.

Go through the gate at the end of the lane and follow the track along the right-hand side of a field (signed 'Coast Path to Ilfracombe'). To the left you now get a good view out to sea and back along the coast, past **Lee** to **Bull Point**. Soon another superb view opens up ahead, with **Ilfracombe** in the distance.

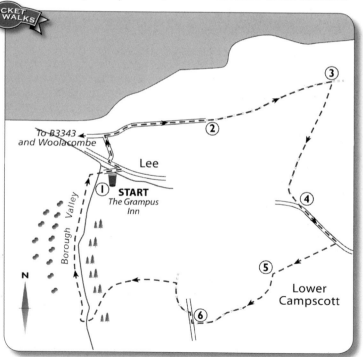

Devon

The charming village of Lee.

3 Soon after your first glimpse of this view, and about ½ mile after leaving the lane, look out for some steps and a public footpath sign on the right. Turn off here, climb the steps, and cross a stile. Go diagonally right across a field to some steps across a wall and, on the other side, bear left to a ladder stile. Cross the next field to another ladder stile onto a track. (There is now another excellent view to the right over Lee and ahead across the fields and woods.) Go through a gate and continue along the track as it swings right and then left. Go through a gate, cross a farmyard to a second gate, and then follow a track to a road.

4 Bear left and, after 350 yards, as the road curves left, turn right through a gate, following the public footpath sign. Cross another farmyard to a gate, and bear right across a field to a stile, some steps and another stile in quick succession. Bear left across the next field and cross a stile on the left to a concrete track.

5 After a few yards, at the entrance to **Lower Campscott Farm**, turn left along an unsurfaced track, following the yellow waymark (there is a sign for **Middle Campscott**, but it is rather hidden).

Cross a stile and a track; then cross a stile and follow the track on the other side along the left-hand side of a field. Do not go through the gate at the end; instead turn right, keeping the field boundary on your left. You pass some farm buildings and cross a stile onto a track. After a few yards go through a gate on the left and turn right onto a track.

5 At its end, go through a gate onto a lane and turn right. When the lane swings right, go straight on through a gate and along a track past some farm buildings to another gate. Follow the track for a short distance and then turn left along a wall (signed to **Borough Valley**). Cross a stile and keep to the left of a field, through gorse and bushes. When the wall turns left, go half left. In the far corner of the field, cross a stile into a conifer plantation. Go down to cross a track, following the yellow waymark, and go down some steps. Cross another track and continue downhill, now along a track rather than a path. At the bottom, turn right off the track to cross a footbridge and go through a gate into broadleaf woodland. Turn right along the path; at the junction after a few yards go right (signed to **Lee**) and cross a stile. This is a lovely stretch, with dense woods all around and a stream gurgling along beside you. After a little over ½ mile you leave the wood via a footbridge and a stile. Keep to the right of the field beyond, cross another stile, and then turn right along a path. This leads to a lane and you will find the **Grampus Inn** on your right.

Places of interest nearby

Near Ilfracombe, 3 miles east of Lee, is 1,000-year-old **Chambercombe Manor**, a place of mystery and legend. It boasts a secret passage and a haunted room. Guided tours of the house are available or you can just wander around the delightful grounds.
☎ 01271 862624

2 Countisbury

The Exmoor Sandpiper Inn

Countisbury **is little more** than a few farms, a pub and an attractive church, but its situation makes it a popular setting-out point for walkers. It is not far from the coast on the northern edge of Exmoor, with paths leading out in all directions: north and west along the coast, east across the moorland and south to the thickly wooded valley of the East Lyn river. This route follows the Coast Path north and then east along the cliff tops, with wonderful views both along the coast and across the Bristol Channel to Wales. After passing through a lovely wood, it turns back across the moorland to Countisbury.

Distance – 4¼ miles.

OS Explorer OL9 Exmoor. GR 747496.
Clear paths and tracks, mainly level but with a few steady climbs.

Starting point The Exmoor Sandpiper Inn. There is usually no objection to customers leaving their cars in the car park while walking, but please ask first. Alternatively, there is a National Trust car park at Barna Barrow, about ¼ mile to the east, which you pass towards the end of the walk, and which involves starting at point 4 on the route.

How to get there The pub is on the A39 between Porlock and Lynmouth, about 1½ miles from the latter.

THE PUB The **Exmoor Sandpiper Inn** dates back to the 13th century and was once a row of cottages; it was not a pub until 1800. Since then it has had three names: the Blue Ball, the Blue Boar and, finally, the Exmoor Sandpiper. It is a long, fairly narrow building with the thick walls and small windows of the original cottages, and is divided into three rooms: two bars and a restaurant, each with its own fireplace. There is also a patio outside. It is a very welcoming place, with a wide range of food, from jacket potatoes and ploughman's lunches to shepherd's pie, Devon lamb chops, and a mouth-watering array of specials, including fresh fish every day.

Open from 11 am to 11 pm every day.
☎ 01598 741263

1 Walk through the pub car park and up the track on the opposite side. Go through a gate into **Countisbury churchyard** and

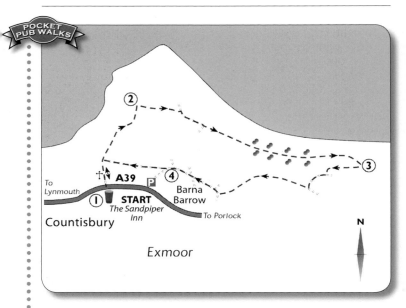

POCKET
PUB WALKS

② ③ ④ ①

To
Lynmouth

✝ A39 P

START
The Sandpiper
Inn

Barna
Barrow

To Porlock

Countisbury

Exmoor

N

follow the path round the church to another gate. The path on the other side takes you alongside a wall. When the wall goes to the right, go straight on along a path. (There is a superb view to your left along the coast to **Lynmouth**, and **Lynton** perched on the hillside above it.) The path climbs to the right, passing a stone hut. You then come to a wall; go left and follow it down. (You now get a very good view to your right along the coast, and ahead you can see the coastline of **Wales** on a clear day, with the **Brecon Beacons** rising above it.) When the wall goes right, go straight on, following the **Coast Path** sign to **Porlock**. After another 300 yards the path goes right (signed to the lighthouse). It clings to the side of a hill, with a scree slope on the other side of the valley and a mass of heather in between the scree. Swing right to follow **Coddow Combe** (there is another scree slope on the other side), before turning left. Some steps then take you down to a surfaced track.

2 Turn right, cross a stream and follow the track up the other side. There is a good variety of wild flowers on either side as you go. After about 200 yards, as the track turns sharp right, go straight on along an unsurfaced track, following the **Coast Path** sign for **Porlock** as it goes round to the right to a gate and stile. On the other side leave it to climb some steps to the right and then to the left, following the **Coast Path** sign. The path now runs along the side of the hill, in and out of some trees, before entering **Chubhill Wood**, a beautiful oakwood stretching up and down the steep slope on either side of you. After about ½ mile, the path leaves the wood through a gate. It then climbs again, now with a mass of rhododendrons on either side, and you get a very good view along the coast ahead, and again across the **Bristol Channel** to **Wales**.

3 Roughly ¼ mile after leaving the wood, you come to a junction; go sharp right here (signed to **Countisbury and County Gate**).

Looking towards Lynmouth from Countisbury.

The path climbs and bends to the left and then to the right. At a track by a wall, turn right and follow it to a gate. On the other side, bear right off the track, following the signpost to **Countisbury**. Go through a gate at the end of a field and cross to a third gate. The path curves round the next field to yet another gate. Cross the following field to the corner of a fence and follow it round a farm. When you reach the surfaced track (signed to **Countisbury**), follow it for a few yards and then, when it turns right to the farm, bear left to an unsurfaced track, following the footpath sign. After a short distance, bear left up a grassy track, again following the footpath sign. Go through a gate and follow the track on the other side. When you come to another surfaced track, bear right and then left, following the sign for **Countisbury**. At the fork go left.

4 After 200 yards there is another fork; go left here if you have parked at **Barna Barrow**, but straight on for the pub. When you come to a junction alongside a wall, go straight on (signed to **Countisbury**). Then, when the main track swings right, go straight on along a slightly narrower track, still following the wall. The track descends, offering a view across **Lynmouth** to **Lynton** again. When the wall turns to the left, follow it round to a gate into the churchyard: this is the way you set out. Follow the path round the church to a gate and go down the track to the car park.

Places of interest nearby

At Lynmouth, 1½ miles west of Countisbury, there is the spectacular **Glen Lyn Gorge**, containing waterfalls, a water wheel and a water cannon. ☎ 01598 752529

Also at Lynmouth is the **Exmoor Brass Rubbing Centre**, which offers instruction as well as brasses to work on. ☎ 01598 752529

The Village Inn

Westward Ho! is said to be the only place in the world with an exclamation mark in its name. It was established as a watering hole in the late 19th century, following the publication of Charles Kingsley's novel of that name, which included many local scenes. This walk takes you from the edge of the village out into the surrounding countryside, with a superb panorama of the hills and valleys around Bideford, and returns along the Coast Path, with more breathtaking views, this time along the coast and out to sea.

THE PUB The main bar of the **Village Inn**, a pleasant Victorian establishment, is carpeted and decorated with local photographs, and has a tiled open fireplace. To one side of it is a games room and, to the other, a light and airy conservatory, attractively decorated. There is a tastefully furnished restaurant with its own bar, and outside there is a sunny, peaceful courtyard. The menu ranges from soups, sandwiches and jacket potatoes to favourites like chicken and chips. In addition, a variety of daily specials is on offer, including roast beef and various French delicacies.

Open from 11 am to 11 pm, Monday to Saturday, and from noon to 10.30 pm on Sunday.
☎ *01237 477331*

Distance – 3¾ miles.

OS Explorer 139 Bideford, Ilfracombe and Barnstaple. GR 432290.
Easy paths and lanes, with just one steep but short hill near the start and a gentler climb a little further on.

Starting point The Village Inn, just off Atlantic Way, Westward Ho! There is no objection to customers leaving their cars in the car park while walking, but please ask first. There is also parking in Atlantic Way.

How to get there Coming from the east on the A39, just outside Bideford, take the A386 north and branch off onto the B3236, following the signs for Westward Ho! From the west, turn off the A39 directly onto the B3236 before the Bideford turning. The B3236 runs along Atlantic Way above the village centre. The Village Inn is in Youngaton Road, just off Atlantic Way.

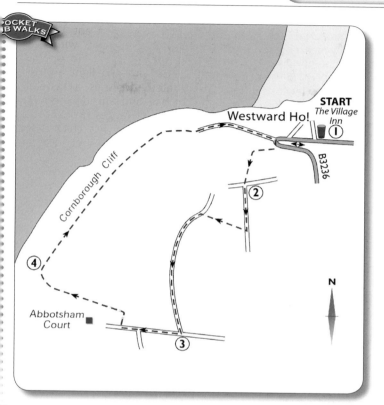

Go to **Atlantic Way** and turn right. Follow the road round as it turns sharp left to leave the village. When, after a few yards, it turns sharp left again, turn right along a drive, following the public footpath sign. (The sea views start immediately if you look out to your right over the holiday complexes of Westward Ho!) When the drive ends, follow a path beside some garages. This leads into a small wooded area. After 200 yards or so you will see the National Trust sign for **Kipling Tors**. Turn left alongside it to climb a steep hill, with steps to ease the way. At the path junction, turn left. You leave the wood and cross a surfaced path, finally emerging through a gate onto a road.

2 Cross the road to a lane and follow it down a gentle hill, with an excellent view ahead over farms and woods. You pass a house and, 50 yards further on, come to a public footpath sign. Turn right and go over a stile into a field, which you cross to a narrow gateway. Bear right across the next field to two stiles and then go right again to a gate onto a lane. Turn left and follow the lane as it winds past a heliport. It then descends a little and climbs gently to a T-junction.

3 Turn right. (There are now good views across the hedges on either side.) At the junction in 300 yards go straight on. When you come to the entrance to **Abbotsham Court**, turn right along a track (signed to **Abbotsham Cliff**). Near the end, cross a stile on the left, following the public footpath sign. Keep to a path alongside a track and, where the track ends at a field, continue alongside a fence. (There is now a new view ahead of you, out to sea, and also to the right.) Cross the stile and keep to the left of the field. About halfway along, you will see a public footpath sign pointing right; follow its direction and cross the field to a stile. As you do so, excellent views open up to left and right.

4 Cross the stile and turn right along the **Coast Path** (signed to **Westward Ho!**). (There are some interesting boulder beaches and rock formations down on your left, and you get perhaps the best view yet along the coast ahead of you – a view that stays with you for most of the rest of the walk.) After just over ½ mile, go through a gate. Soon afterwards the coast curves to the right and you can see across **Westward Ho!** to the dunes of **Northam Burrows**. Soon you come to the outskirts of **Westward Ho!**, where you join a road and pass a succession of holiday parks. Follow the road to a T-junction and turn left. You are now back in **Atlantic Way**, and you will find **Youngaton Road** and the **Village Inn** 300 yards further along on the left.

The view across from Westward Ho! to Northam Burrows.

Places of interest nearby

About 3 miles south-west of Westward Ho! is **The Big Sheep**, a working farm combined with plenty of attractions for young and old alike.
☎ 01237 472366

4 **Chittlehamholt**

The Exeter Inn

Tucked into a bend in the River Taw, the surrounds of Chittlehamholt and Warkleigh are one of the hidden gems of mid-Devon. This is an area of rich farmland and beautiful woods, criss-crossed by paths and green lanes, and with outstanding views to the south. The walk takes you west from Chittlehamholt to the Forestry Commission's Shortridge Wood. A green lane then runs north to the neighbouring hamlet of Warkleigh. From there farm paths and a little-used lane take you down to the Taw Valley, where you join another green lane for the return leg.

THE PUB

Dating from the 15th century, The **Exeter Inn** once served the packhorse trains that travelled between Barnstaple and Exeter. This lovely thatched hostelry now offers a warm welcome to locals and visitors alike. The entrance leads straight into the stone-floored bar, which is separated from the carpeted lounge by wooden dividers. There is a family room, and at the back is a snug little restaurant. Matchboxes and books decorate the low beams. Outside there are also tables. The food, which is all home cooked, ranges from soups and light meals to specials such as steak and Guinness pie.

Open from 11.30 am to 2.30 pm and from 6 pm to 11 pm, Monday to Saturday; from noon to 3 pm and from 7 pm to 10.30 pm on Sunday.
☎ *01769 540281*

Distance – 5 miles.

OS Explorer 127 South Molton and Chulmleigh.
GR 650208.
Mainly easy tracks, lanes and farm paths, but with a few climbs.

Starting point The village hall car park in Chittlehamholt. The Exeter Inn's car park is very small, and walkers are asked not to leave their cars there while walking, but the village hall is only 100 yards along the road to the south. There is also parking in the road.

How to get there Chittlehamholt is signed to the west of the B3226, which runs between South Molton and the A377.

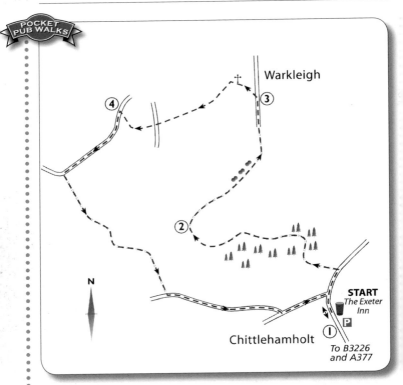

1 Turn right as you leave the car park and pass the pub. At the junction go straight on (signed to **Chittlehampton** and **South Molton**). In 200 yards, when you come to the sign for M & M Plants, turn left through a gate, following the public footpath sign. Follow the track to another gate, and continue along it on the right-hand side of a field. A gate takes you into the Forestry Commission's **Shortridge Wood**. Keep to the track as it descends to the right and to the left. Where it forks, go right to cross a stream. At the next fork, after 200 yards, go right again to climb above a cleared area. When you come to a gate, go to the left

of it, following a path to a stile. Keep to the right of the field, with an excellent view ahead of you across the valley of the **River Taw**. Cross another stile and go to the right of a house and through a gate onto a green lane.

The lane climbs gently for almost ½ mile and then descends past a wood to a stream. Cross a small footbridge and follow the green lane as it climbs to the left on the other side. After 200 yards it comes out at a lane; go straight on for 300 yards and look out for a public footpath sign on the left, just before the lane bends to the right.

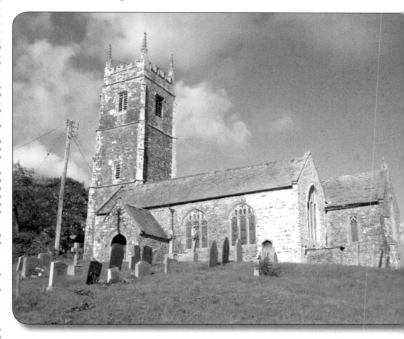

The church of St John at Warkleigh.

3. Go down the path to a gate and bear slightly right down a field to cross a small stream. Climb up the other side, enjoying the outstanding view to your left. Skirt round **Warkleigh churchyard** and then a house. Just beyond it, go left to a small gate and turn immediately right to another gate. Go through it and turn left to follow the hedge, carrying straight on across the field when the hedge goes left. You will see three gaps in the hedge ahead of you; aim for the one in the middle, and cross a stile alongside a trough. There is now a beautiful view ahead of you. Bear slightly left across a field to a gate leading into a lane. Cross the lane to a gate and then keep to the left of the next field to go through another gate. Then go right, to a stile. As you do so, you will see the ruins of **Little Shortridge House** on your left. Cross the next field to a gate into a lane.

4. Turn left and follow the lane as it descends steeply into the valley. After ½ mile, just as the lane swings right, go left along a surfaced drive, following the public bridleway sign, which takes you to a farmyard. Go through the yard and follow the surfaced track at the other side. When you come to a house called **Cleave Copse**, go along the green lane to the right of it. At the fork go left, following the blue bridleway waymark, and at the next junction, after 300 yards, follow the green lane round to the right. It climbs for about 300 yards and comes out at a lane; turn left here. The lane also climbs, and after a little over ½ mile there is a T-junction, where you turn left to reach Chittlehamholt. At the T-junction in the village go left to return to the start.

Places of interest nearby

About 4½ miles to the north-west is the **Cobbaton Combat Collection**, a comprehensive collection of militaria.
☎ 01769 540740

5 Chulmleigh

The Globe

Chulmleigh is a charming old hilltop town overlooking the valleys of the Little Dart and Taw rivers, and this is very much a hill and valley walk – indeed, for part of the way it follows a longer route known as the Ridge and Valley Walk. There are outstanding views across the two valleys and some lovely stretches of woodland, both coniferous and deciduous. On an ancient track, you go down to the Little Dart and through conifer plantations, crossing some little streams as you go. The return leg takes you across fields to a deciduous wood, where you cross the Little Dart again before following its valley back to Chulmleigh.

Distance – 5½ miles.

OS Explorer 127 South Molton and Chulmleigh.
GR 686141.
Clear paths, with plenty of ups and downs. Be prepared for some muddy patches.

Starting point The church in the centre of Chulmleigh. The pub is next to the church, but has no car park. However, there is free parking on both sides of the church, that on the south side being slightly more convenient.

How to get there Take the B3096 east from the A377 Crediton to Barnstaple road.

THE PUB

The **Globe** is a delightful little pub down a narrow cul-de-sac next to the church. There is a comfortable, carpeted lounge, with an open fireplace at one end; separated by a wooden partition is a small, cosy dining alcove. The public bar has a pool table and games, and a wood-burning stove to keep the cold at bay in winter. There are also a few tables outside, alongside the 13th century church. The lunchtime menu offers sandwiches and jacket potatoes, as well as more substantial meals such as Cumberland sausage and chilli con carne. The evening menu is more extensive and adventurous. All the food is locally sourced and freshly cooked.

Open from 11.30 am to 3 pm and from 5.30 pm to 11 pm, Monday to Friday, and all day on Saturday and Sunday.
☎ 01769 580252

1 If you have parked to the south of the church, follow the lane you are on away from the main street, and just before it turns

right, turn off left down a steep surfaced track marked **Rock Hill**. If you have parked on the north side, follow the lane away from the main street and then go round to the left and turn left again to locate Rock Hill on your right. Follow it downhill; at the bottom of the hill it narrows to a path. Cross a footbridge over the **Little Dart** river and follow the track that climbs up the other side of the valley. You come out onto a track at a farm; turn left here soon to join a surfaced lane, with a very good view to the right. After 200 yards, go straight on at the crossroads (signed to **Eggesford Station** and **Crediton**).

This lane goes down steeply and curves to the left through a wood. Just before it bends right, turn left, following the public footpath sign for **Eggesford Forest**. Go through a gate and

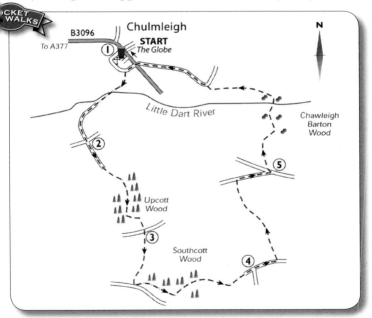

The Little Dart river.

bear right across the field. You will see two gaps in the hedge ahead of you; aim for the one on the left. Cross a small footbridge and then a stile, and enter **Upcott Wood**. Follow the track straight ahead as it winds through the conifers for about 500 yards. At the end, go through a gate, then left through another gate, and immediately right up some steps into another section of the wood. Follow the path through the trees to a road.

3 Turn right and, after a short distance, go left, following the public footpath sign for **Eggesford Forest** again. Keep to the left of the field, and at the end go through the gate just to the right. Follow the grassy track that winds down the hill towards the stream. Cross a stile at the end of the field and follow a path to a drive, which leads you to the A377. Turn left; after two or three yards, turn left again into **Southcott Wood**. Take the track that runs parallel to the road, following the public bridleway sign for **Southcott**. It climbs out of the valley, skirting the wood, and you get a lovely view up the **River Taw**. Towards the top the route swings left into the wood, which you leave via a gate in 500 yards. Bear right across the field ahead to the far right-hand corner. (To your right is a superb view across to Dartmoor.) Go through the gateway and past a farm to a cattle grid.

4 Follow the lane on the other side, and at the junction go straight on (signed to **Chawley**). 200 yards further on you will see a public footpath sign on the left. Cross the stile and cut across to a gate. Follow the right-hand boundary of the field beyond. Go

through a gate and bear left across the field ahead to a stile, two footbridges and another stile in quick succession. Having crossed these, follow the track up the field and go through a gate at the top. Then follow the hedge-line round to the right. At the end of that field, go through a gate onto the B3042 and turn right. After ¼ mile, at the junction with B3096, turn left.

In a few yards, turn right down a track and immediately left through a gate. (*The footbridge across the Little Dart river, about ½ mile along this path, was down at the time of writing, but due to be repaired by July 2007. If a notice at the entrance to the track indicates that the repairs are still be be completed, continue along the B3096 to return to Chulmleigh.*) Cross a field to a gateway and keep to the left of the next field. At the end, follow the boundary round to the right and go through another gateway onto a track. Bear left down a hill and enter a wood. When the track forks, go right and continue your descent through the wood. After 150 yards or so, look out for a yellow waymark pointing right, which you follow along a path through a small conifer plantation and across a track. Keep to the path through the closely planted trees for the short distance to the **Little Dart** river. Cross the footbridge and the field beyond. Then turn left and follow the hedge to a gap in a bank. Bear right in the next field to a stile, two footbridges and another stile in quick succession. Turn left in the field that follows and a stile takes you into a lane. Bear left here and follow the lane as it climbs steeply out of the valley. After ¾ mile you will find yourself back in **Chulmleigh**. At the junction in the centre, turn right, and then left for the car park.

Places of interest nearby

About 4 miles south of Chulmleigh, just off the A377, is **Eggesford Gardens**, a country park and garden centre.
☎ 01769 580250

The Hartnoll Country House Hotel

The Exe Valley is an area of scattered woods, rolling hills and extensive views. This delightful amble takes you from the picturesque village of Bolham up a hillside, along flower-filled lanes, green lanes and tracks, with some lovely views across the valley as you go. The return leg is through a wood to the National Trust's Knightshayes Court estate, providing an opportunity to visit this fascinating Victorian country house. A pretty lane brings you back to Bolham.

Distance – 3½ miles.

OS Explorer 114 Exeter and the Exe Valley. GR 951148. Generally easy going, along lanes and green lanes, with just one steady but fairly gentle climb near the start.

Starting point The Hartnoll Country House Hotel. The owner has no objection to customers leaving their cars in the hotel car park while they walk, but please ask first. There is also a car park across the main road in the village. If you decide to visit Knightshayes Court, you might prefer to start your walk from there (point 5).

How to get there *The hotel is right on the A396, ½ mile north of its junction with the A361 North Devon link road at Tiverton.*

THE PUB

The **Hartnoll** has had a varied history. It started out as the dower house of nearby Knightshayes Court, became a school between the wars, and was then converted into a hotel. The public rooms comprise a cosy bar, furnished with comfortable armchairs, a conservatory, and a restaurant (open for lunch and dinner) overlooking a stream. Outside is a large garden extending down to the stream. The menu caters for all tastes, and includes excellent-value bar snacks like ploughman's lunches, sandwiches and 'toasties', as well as meat, fish and vegetarian main meals and daily specials, all using local produce where possible. And because of the extended opening hours, you can pop in for refreshments at almost any time, whether for breakfast or a late-night snack.

Open from 7 am to 2 am.
☎ *01885 252777*

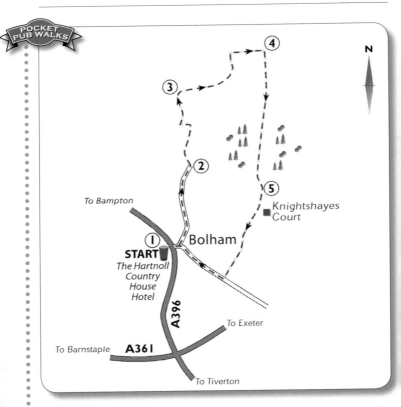

1 Cross the road to the village and follow the lane round to the right. Go under a bridge and turn left immediately beyond it into another lane, which passes some cottages and climbs gently, winding slightly as it goes. You pass a wood on the left and continue climbing.

2 About ½ mile after leaving Bolham, you will see a private drive to **Knightshayes Court** on the right. Bear left onto a concrete track, which continues to climb for a while and then begins to

descend. (Before the descent, look to the left for a good view across the **Exe Valley**.) At the bottom of a short hill the track turns sharp left across a little valley and climbs again on the other side, ending at a farm. Now go to the right of the house to a rough track, which becomes a broad green lane and swings to the left, getting narrower. The hedgerows on either side are filled with wild flowers in season.

At the top of the hill, go through a gate and then keep to the top edge of the field. Look back for an excellent view across the valley to the rolling hills beyond. At the end of the field go

The stable block at Knightshayes.

through a gate and keep to the top of the next field. After a few yards you will find hedges on either side, and the path then goes in and out of hedges for a while, always skirting the top of the field. At the end go through a gate and turn left along a green lane. When you get to a farmyard, turn right along a track.

4 After 300 yards turn right at the T-junction and follow the attractive flower-lined track for almost ½ mile to a wood. At this point it becomes a surfaced lane, which descends through the wood, with high banks on either side. After ¼ mile go through a gate into the **Knightshayes** estate. Passing the walled kitchen garden on your left, you come to a T-junction, with the old stable block on your left. Turn right onto the main drive.

5 Look to the right for a magnificent view across the Exe Valley. The drive leads you round to the right, past Knightshayes Court itself, and through the park to the main gate. At the lane, turn right (signed to **Bolham and Tiverton**). The view over the valley is now half left. Follow the lane to Bolham and cross the main road to return to the hotel.

Places of interest nearby

Knightshayes Court is richly decorated with the work of William Burges. With its well-tended gardens, which include a large walled garden, and rolling parkland, it is certainly worth a visit in its own right.
☎ 01884 254665

In Tiverton, a mile to the south, is **Tiverton Castle**, which dates back 900 years.
☎ 01884 255200

7 Halwill Junction

The Junction Inn

As its name suggests, Halwill Junction was an important railway junction until the line was axed in the Beeching cuts of the 1960s. It is now a popular venue for anglers, with a number of fishing lakes nearby, some of which are encountered on this route. Passing the Winsford Centre (built in 1899 as a cottage hospital and designed by the celebrated Victorian architect, Charles Annesley Voysey), the walk takes you out along a little-used lane full of flowers and wildlife before cutting across to the open spaces of Hollow Moor. The return leg crosses the moor, meanders through a wood, and then follows a delightful track past the fishing lakes and the Forestry Commission's Winsford Plantation. There are some excellent views along the way, including some of Dartmoor.

Devon

Distance – 3¾ miles.

OS Explorer 112 Launceston and Holsworthy. GR 444000. Mainly lanes and tracks; with some rough moorland in the middle section.

Starting point The Junction Inn at Halwill Junction. There is no objection to customers leaving their cars in the pub car park, as long as they ask. Otherwise there is a car park by the old station, and another alongside the parish hall.

How to get there Halwill Junction is on the A3079 between Okehampton and Holsworthy. The Junction Inn is just off the main road to the east.

THE PUB The **Junction Inn** is a friendly pub, full of atmosphere. It has one large, panelled bar, decorated with old railway photographs, with a little snug off it. There are window seats and a wood-burning stove. Outside, there are tables and benches on an attractive, sheltered terrace and also at the front. The food, which is all home-cooked, and locally sourced wherever possible, ranges from jacket potatoes to steaks, fish and daily specials such as battered chicken.

Open from 11 am to 2.30 pm and 6 pm to 11 pm, Monday to Thursday; from 11 am to 11 pm on Friday and Saturday; and noon to 11 pm on Sunday.
☎ 01409 221239

---

1 Turn left from the pub into a lane marked 'No through road'. Almost immediately, you pass the **Winsford Centre** and soon you get a splendid view to the right. After a few twists, the lane runs straight for some distance, with good views over the hedges

on either side. It is very peaceful, with no traffic, and just the breeze in the trees and occasional birdsong to break the silence.

After 1½ miles you will find the entrance to **Leasefield** ahead of you; turn left along a concrete track. Follow it past a house to a farmyard and cross to a gate. Go through another gate into a field, which you cross to a gate that leads you onto **Hollow Moor**, a wide expanse of sedge and long grass, with very good views ahead. Turn left along a broad track where the grass has been cleared. When it swings left, cut across the grass to a gap in the belt of trees ahead. Make your way through the long grass on the other side towards a wood, crossing two more cleared tracks as you go. Go through the gate marked with a blue bridleway waymark that leads into the wood.

Follow the woodland path as it winds among the trees. Cross a cleared area and then follow a narrow path, which takes you to a gate, where you leave the wood and cross a stream. Bear left on the other side along a path between banks, which takes you onto a track. You will find fishing lakes on either side of you, and

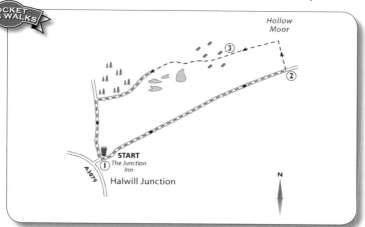

Hollow Moor

START
The Junction Inn
Halwill Junction

A3079

N

The view from Hollow Moor.

soon you come to some houses and **Winsford Walled Garden**. You pass through a complex of holiday cottages, and the track becomes a surfaced lane. To the left is a panoramic view across to Dartmoor. Skirt the Forestry Commission's **Winsford Plantation** on your right, and emerge at a road. Turn left and follow the road for about ½ mile to **Halwill Junction**. The pub is on the left.

Places of interest nearby

Winsford Walled Garden, which you pass on the walk, is a beautifully preserved Victorian garden with over 3,000 varieties of plant. It is open to the public in summer.
☎ 01409 221477

The White Hart

This delightful walk takes you along flower-filled lanes and green lanes, with the occasional woodland and farm path to add variety. En route you can enjoy some outstanding views over the mid-Devon countryside to Dartmoor. You follow the valley of the River Taw, the playground of the otter in Henry Williamson's classic story of *Tarka the Otter* (in fact part of the walk follows the Tarka Trail, a long-distance route that links many of the places associated with the book) to the charming hamlet of Bondleigh. The return is across farms and through woods, with a wander through the bustling little town of North Tawton to finish.

Distance – 4¾ miles.

OS Explorer 113 Okehampton. GR 661017.
Lanes, green lanes and easy farm and woodland paths, with one or two hills.

Starting point The White Hart, in Fore Street, North Tawton. There is no pub car park, but there is parking in the street.

How to get there Turn north off the A3072 between Okehampton and Crediton, following the signs for North Tawton. Follow the road through the town, and you will find the White Hart on the right.

THE PUB The **White Hart** has an interesting layout. You enter through an arch in the rather plain frontage and find yourself in a courtyard, with a colourful patio beer garden straight ahead. The first room on the left is the restaurant (open in the evenings only), followed by the bar. Around the bar itself is a flagstone floor and beyond it lies an area with a wooden floor and tables, comfortable armchairs and a wood-burning stove, which is open to the roof, with enormous beams across. Behind that is a games room. The menu ranges from jacket potatoes and sandwiches to main courses such as Cumberland sausage, beef Bourguignon, and a hearty all-day breakfast.

Open from 11 am to 11 pm, Monday to Friday; and from 10 am to midnight on Saturday and Sunday.
☎ *01837 82473*

1 Turn right along **Fore Street**. After a short distance, turn right again to go up a green lane, following the public footpath sign.

As you come to a gate on the left, look through it for a great view across to Dartmoor. At the top of the green lane, go through a gate and turn right along another green lane. When you come to a gate, follow the green lane round to the left. It soon swings right and left again, and after 100 yards or so you cross two stiles, looking left as you do so for another excellent view, this time over rolling farmland. Continue along the green lane ahead and at its end, cross two stiles and keep to the left of a field to a gate on the left. Bear right diagonally across the next field to a gate. Go through it and turn right; after a short distance you will come to a stile on the right.

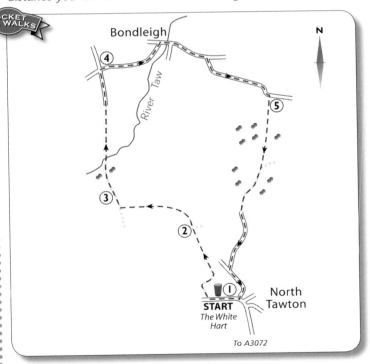

POCKET WALKS

Bondleigh

N

River Taw

④
⑤
③
②
①

START
The White Hart

North Tawton

To A3072

Devon

2️⃣ After crossing the stile turn left into a green lane. Cross two stiles in quick succession to continue along the green lane. It is very quiet and tranquil here, with only the occasional bird call for company. The green lane ends at a gate, which you go through; then straight across the long field ahead. When you meet a track coming in from the left, follow it until it swings left to a gate; at this point go straight on for a few yards to a stile. Go round to the left

The clock tower in North Tawton.

of the next field to a stile leading to a path between hedges. Pass through a gate and follow the path to the left and then to the right, round some houses. Go down some steps and turn left to a track; now turn right.

3️⃣ At the junction after a few yards, go straight on, following the sign for the unmetalled road. At the next junction also keep straight on. This is another very pretty stretch, with trees all around, and it leads to the **River Taw**. Cross the footbridge and on the other side go straight on (signed to **Bondleigh**). You are now on the **Tarka Trail**, a broad, easy track between high banks and hedges, which winds and climbs gently for about 600 yards, ending at a surfaced lane. Keep straight on, enjoying the fine view to your right.

4 Another ¼ mile will bring you to a junction, where you turn right (signed to **Bondleigh**). At the T-junction ½ mile further on, turn right to cross the **River Taw** again (signed to **North Tawton**). This is where you leave the Tarka Trail. At the junction on the other side of the bridge, go straight on, climbing out of the valley. At the top, turn right at the junction (signed to **Hill**). The lane swings left and then climbs. (Look back for further view of the rich farmland and of Dartmoor beyond, on the right.) The lane swings right past a farm; when it swings left again, go straight on through a gate, following the public footpath sign.

5 Bear slightly right across a field to a stile, which leads you into a wood. Follow the clear path through the wood to a stile and continue through some scrub on the other side. Cross a footbridge and follow the path along the edge of the wood. Go over the stile at the end and keep left as you cross the field beyond. Now go through a gate on the left, following the yellow waymark, and walk down to a broad green lane; turn right here. You pass a pond on the left and enter a wood. Go through a gate at the end of the wood and then continue along the green lane. It ends at a surfaced lane; go straight on. At the T-junction in 700 yards, turn left to return to **North Tawton**. When you get to **The Square** in the town centre, turn right along **Fore Street** to the pub.

Places of interest nearby

At Okehampton, about 7 miles south-west of North Tawton, is the **Museum of Dartmoor Life**.
☎ 01837 52295.
Also in Okehampton are the remains of **Okehampton Castle**, dating back to the Normans.
☎ 01837 52844

9 Stockland

The King's Arms Inn

This is an exploration of an exceptionally beautiful yet largely hidden part of East Devon. Stockland is a picturesque village on the slopes of the Yarty Valley and, as you follow the route up the hillside behind it, breathtaking views of the valley below open up, with rolling green hills and a patchwork of fields and woods. There is a lovely woodland stretch along the way, and on the way back you pass the prehistoric earthworks of Stockland Little Castle.

THE PUB Despite its rather plain exterior, the **King's Arms** is a lovely, 16th century inn, with exposed stone walls and low black beams. Next to the bar, with its attractive flagstone floor, is a carpeted lounge, furnished with armchairs. Round the corner is what they call the restaurant bar, which has an enormous open fireplace at one end and a smaller one at the other, and a panelled divide in between. There is a cosy dining room, also with a large fireplace which is open only in the evening and at Sunday lunchtime. The menu ranges from soups, salads and ploughman's lunches to fish, game, meat and vegetarian main courses.

Open from noon to 3 pm and from 6.30 pm to 11.30 pm.
☎ *01404 881361*

Distance – 3½ miles.

OS Explorer 116 Lyme Regis and Bridport. GR 244046. Mostly clear paths and lanes, but one section liable to be muddy and one that can become overgrown (stout shoes and trousers rather than shorts are therefore recommended), and several climbs, one quite steep.

Starting point The King's Arms Inn in Stockland. The landlord has no objection to customers leaving their cars in the pub car park while they walk, but please ask first. Otherwise, there is some parking in the roads through the village.

How to get there Stockland is south of the A30 and north-east of Honiton, and is clearly signed from both. The pub is in the middle of the village.

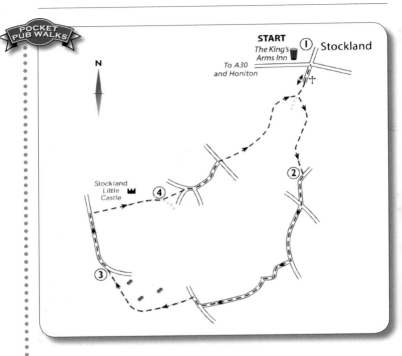

POCKET PUB WALKS

N

START ① Stockland
The King's
Arms Inn
To A30
and Honiton

②

Stockland
Little
Castle ④

③

1 Turn left and after a few yards take the first turning on the right
into a narrow lane, which leads down to the church. Go round
to the right, and, on the other side of the church, go through
the gate leading onto a lane. Keep to the lane until it swings
left; then, instead of following it, go straight on along a track
to a gate. Walk along the left-hand hedge of the field beyond,
crossing a small stream. When you come to a gate on the left, go
through and then turn right. Keep to the right in the next field
and go through the gate at the end (the ground here can be
muddy, so take care). Keep left to a smaller gate leading onto a
green lane, which can be overgrown with brambles and nettles
at times but is quite passable.

In about 300 yards a stile takes you into a lane, where you turn right. At the junction a few yards further on, go straight on and also at the crossroads 200 yards ahead. You now get an excellent view ahead over rolling farmland. After ¼ mile turn right down a lane (signed to **Ford**). The lane swings left past a farm and then right again, crossing a stream and then climbing out of the valley. At the T-junction near the top, turn right (signed to **Millhayes**). After a few yards turn left up a track, but before you do so look right for a view across the valley of the **River Yarty**. The track enters a delightful wooded stretch and then swings right. When it forks, go left to follow the edge of more woodland.

You emerge onto a lane by a farm; go straight on. After about ¼ mile you will come to two public footpath signs, one pointing left and the other right; turn right through a gate, and keep

The entrance to the church of St Michael & All Angels, Stockland.

to the right of the field beyond. About halfway down the field you will see a gate on the right; go through it and keep to the left of the next field. A lovely view down the valley opens up here. Beyond the hedge on your left you will see the earthworks of prehistoric **Stockland Little Castle** (so-called to distinguish it from Stockland Great Castle, which is about ½ mile to the south). At the end of the field, go through the gate into a green lane. When the green lane swings right to a gate, go through a gate on the left and turn right to go diagonally across a field to a stile into a lane.

4 Turn left and, at the junction a few yards ahead, follow the main lane round to the right. At the next junction keep to the main lane again. You cross a stream and then climb steeply out of the valley. At the T-junction at the top, turn right and after about 50 yards you will see a public footpath sign on the left. Go through the gate and straight across the field beyond to a gateway. Cut across the next field to a gap in a hedge, and in the next field go to the right and follow the boundary round to the left. At the field end, go right through a gate and straight across to the far left-hand side of the next field. Here you will rejoin the track you set out on. Follow it to the lane and then go round the church to join the lane on the other side. At the top turn left to return to the pub.

Places of interest nearby

Five miles south of Stockland, near Dalwood, are **Burrow Farm Gardens**, 7 acres of landscaped gardens.
☎ 01404 831285

The Drewe Arms

Drewsteignton **is a lovely** little village on the edge of Dartmoor, overlooking the spectacular Teign Gorge. It is believed to take its name from a Norman knight, Drogo de Teigne, who was the local landowner. Thatched cottages surround the central square, with the imposing 15th and 16th century church at one end. This route takes you along a green lane and farm paths to join the Hunters' Path, high above the

Distance – 2¼ miles

OS Explorer OL28 Dartmoor. GR 735908.
A short climb near the start, but otherwise easy walking along clear paths and tracks.

Starting point The Square in Drewsteignton. The pub car park is very small, and the licensee asks walkers not to leave their cars there while walking. There is, however, plenty of parking in The Square or in the car park on the road out of the village towards Exeter.

How to get there The village lies south of the A30 Exeter to Okehampton road and east of the A382, between Moretonhampstead and Whiddon Down, and is signed from both directions.

gorge, with spectacular views across the river to Dartmoor. The Hunters' Path leads into a beautiful wood, full of birdsong, and a track brings you full circle, through a conifer plantation, to the village.

THE PUB The **Drewe Arms** is a gem of a pub. During the last century, it had the longest-serving landlady in the country in 'Aunty' Mabel Mudge, who held the licence from 1919 to 1994, retiring only when she was well into her nineties. It still retains much of its character. There is no counter, just two serving hatches. There is a small public bar on the left as you enter and an equally small lounge across the main entrance passage. Both are decorated with old photographs, many featuring 'Aunty Mabel', and the lounge has a welcoming fire in winter. Down a side passage is Aunty Mabel's Kitchen, a pretty little restaurant, which, as its name suggests, was converted from the original kitchen and still has an old range at one end. A wide selection of locally sourced food is on offer, from the ploughman's platters (including trout, duck and salmon, as well as the more usual cheese and ham), to soups, pies and a variety of specials.

Open from 11 am to 3 pm and from 6 pm to midnight (all day on Friday, Saturday and Sunday in summer).
☎ *01647 281224*

Turn left out of **The Square** and, at the junction in a few yards, follow the main lane round to the right (signed to **Whiddon Down**, **Moretonhampstead**, **Chagford** and **Castle Drogo**). On the edge of the village, turn left down a green lane (signed to the Hunters' Path, Fingle Bridge and the road near Castle Drogo). As

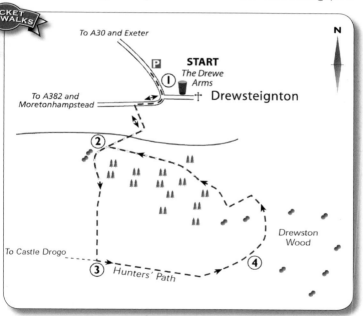

Devon

The view up the Teign Valley.

you progress the lane becomes almost a tunnel, with the trees on either side meeting overhead. You come to two gates and swing right to descend to a stream.

2 At the junction, go straight on (signed to the **Hunters' Path**), following the path as it climbs and narrows when it enters a wood. It is very pretty here, with a stream running down on your right. Towards the top the climb becomes steeper, but there are steps to help you. Go through a gate and follow the right-hand edge of a field, still climbing but more gently now. Look to the right and behind you for a broad view across the woods and fields. Cross a stile and keep to the right. Now an even more spectacular view opens up ahead and to the right, to the barren slopes of Dartmoor. Cross another stile and go down to meet the **Hunters' Path**.

Turn left here (signed to **Drewsteignton** (indirect) and **Fingle Bridge**). (Alternatively, you can turn right for a detour of about a mile to **Castle Drogo**; see 'Places of interest nearby' below.) The path takes you high above the River Teign, with a mass of purple heather on the slopes in summer, and the densely wooded valley far below you.

In 600 yards, go straight on at the junction (signed 'Hunters' Path to Drewsteignton'). You now enter **Drewston Wood** and start to descend. With a mass of trees stretching down to the river on the right, it is alive with birdsong. The path curves to the left and continues to descend gently. As you round the hill, the broadleaf woodland gives way to conifers and the path crosses a track. It then swings right to cross a stream and joins another track; bear right here and descend to a junction, where you go straight on (signed to **Drewsteignton**). At the next junction you join the green lane you set out on. Turn right (signed to **Drewsteignton**) and follow it up and round to the left. At the road, turn right and follow it to the left, back to **The Square**.

Places of interest nearby

Castle Drogo is just a mile west of Drewsteignton. Despite its name, it is not really a castle, nor did it belong to anyone called Drogo. It is a large country house built towards the beginning of the 20th century for Julius Drewe, who claimed descent from Drogo de Teigne, a corruption of whose name was believed to be the 'Drewe' of Drewsteignton. Now in the hands of the National Trust, it gives a fascinating insight into life between the wars. It has exquisite gardens, and the views from the front are outstanding.
☎ 01647 433306

The Dolphin Hotel

This magnificent walk takes you from the picturesque old fishing village of Beer, once the haunt of smugglers, along a superb stretch of the Jurassic Coast, a World Heritage Site. You follow the top of the chalk cliffs to the seaside village of Branscombe and return along the South West Coast Path, between the cliffs and the sea. On both the outward and return journeys, the views along the coast are stunning. The rock formations are quite fascinating, and there are opportunities to go down to the long pebble beach for a paddle or a swim.

Distance – 3¾ miles.

OS Explorer 116 Lyme Regis and Bridport. GR 228892. Good paths and tracks; be prepared for a few climbs, some quite steep.

Starting point Dolphin Road in Beer. The hotel car park is for residents only, but there is a pay-and-display car park just behind it, in Dolphin Road.

How to get there *Take the B3174 south from the A3052 Exeter to Lyme Regis road (signed to Beer), then follow the signs for the village centre. The hotel is in Fore Street, on the corner with Dolphin Road, and the car park is behind it.*

THE PUB The **Dolphin Hotel** is believed to be about 200 years old. The public accommodation comprises a very attractive, panelled lounge bar and a more basic public bar. The former has a Victorian fireplace, with a fire in winter, and is decorated with old photographs of Beer, and a variety of maritime knick-knacks. The latter has a pool table. There is a patio at the back of the building. The menu, as one would expect given its location, includes plenty of locally caught fish, but there is also a range of other main courses, as well as sandwiches and ploughman's lunches.

Open from 10 am to 3 pm and from 6 pm to 11 pm (lounge bar) and from 10 am to 1 am (public bar).
☎ *01297 20068*

Follow **Dolphin Road** away from **Fore Street** and take the first turning on the left, along **The Meadows**. At the T-junction turn right, following the sign to a car park. Climb out of the village and look back for the first of the coastal views. At the next junction, go straight on, past the entrance to the car park, and then past a caravan park.

2 At the top of the road cross a cattle grid; when the surfaced road bends right, go straight on across a cattle grid onto a track. Follow the track along the right-hand edge of a long field. (Look back again for an even better view across **Beer Roads**.) Cross a cattle grid at the end and follow the track to the right. Go to the right of two houses. (Another memorable view now opens up in front of you, along the coast to the west.) At the end of a long field go through two gates. When the next field opens up you will come to a junction in the path; go straight on and then

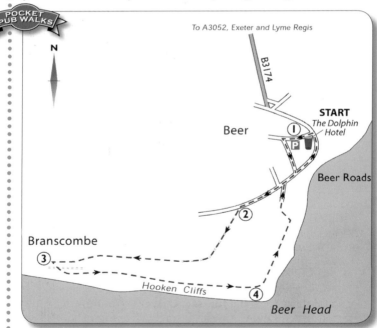

The seaside at Branscombe Mouth.

to the left, down some steep steps. Towards the bottom of the field, cross a stile and keep to the left of the following field to a gate (with a good view of **Branscombe Mouth** and its lovely long stretch of beach). Keep to the left again to meet a concrete track.

3 Here you can take a slight detour straight onto the beach. The main route, however, turns sharp left at the track, following the coast path sign for **Beer**. In the caravan park, go left where the path forks. Near the top of the path, which now climbs, branch right, following the coast path sign for Beer again. This takes you out of the caravan park and through some trees. (From time to time breaks in the trees will give you views on your left of the deeply fissured chalk cliffs towering above you that are a feature of this part of the **Jurassic Coast** and of the long, largely deserted beach below you on the right. Occasionally there are paths going down to it if you would like to make another short detour.) The flower-fringed path goes up and down at times, usually with steps to help you. About ¾ mile after joining the coast path it climbs steeply left. At the top you get an excellent view along the coast, and of some interesting rock formations.

④ The path takes you round **Beer Head**, a wonderful view opening up eastwards, past Seaton to Lyme Bay. Go through a kissing-gate and cross a field to second kissing-gate. The path swings left and crosses a field to a third kissing-gate. Keep to the right of the next field to a fourth kissing-gate and then keep to the right again. A gap in the hedge leads you into another field; keep left to a kissing-gate, which takes you onto a gravel path between hedges. It swings right, past the car park you passed on the way out, and joins a surfaced track. At its end, turn right down **Common Lane**, which leads to **Beer's harbour**, with its reminders of a time when, alongside fishing, smuggling was the mainstay of the village's economy, the caves along the cliffs having provided an ideal hiding place for contraband. Turn left from the harbour into **Fore Street**, and after about 150 yards you will find the **Dolphin Hotel** on the left and **Dolphin Road** just beyond it.

Places of interest nearby

Just outside Beer are two very different attractions. **Pecorama** is a pretty garden, with a miniature train running through it. There is also an exhibition of model trains.
☎ 01297 21542

The **Beer Quarry Caves** are a series of caverns formed from Roman times to the early 20th century by the quarrying of clay. (These too were a perfect place for the smugglers to hide their goods.)
☎ 01297 680282

The White Hart Hotel

Flowery green lanes, open downland, cool woods and tinkling streams – this lovely walk has them all, plus impressive moorland views. On the way out of the delightful little town of Moretonhampstead you pass some attractive 17th century almshouses and then follow farm paths and a green lane to Mardon Down, where the whole of south-eastern Dartmoor is laid out before you. Little-used lanes, more paths and green lanes then bring you back to Moretonhampstead through two woods and along the bank of a gently flowing stream.

 THE PUB

During the Napoleonic Wars, the **White Hart** was a meeting place for officer prisoners of war on parole from Dartmoor Prison. The bar of this 16th century coaching

Devon

inn has low beams, a wooden floor with rugs, and window seats, and is decorated with old prints. There is also an elegant lounge, carpeted and furnished with comfortable armchairs, which is open to non-residents at lunchtime only. Outside is a shady courtyard. The food ranges from open sandwiches and ploughman's lunches to main courses such as quiche, steak and mushroom pie and a variety of fish dishes. There is also a restaurant menu available in the evenings.

Open from 11 am to 11 pm, Monday to Saturday, and from noon to 10.30 pm on Sunday.
☎ *01647 441340*

1 Cross the **A382** to **Cross Street** (signed to Exeter and Dunsford). Soon you will pass a large copper beech on the left. Known as the Cross Tree, it was planted to replace an enormous elm, the Dancing Tree, so called because dances were held on a platform

in its pollarded branches. Just beyond, you can see a row of 17th century almshouses, built of the local granite (the date 1637 is visible above the arch). Turn left just beyond them, through a kissing-gate, into a park. Bear right to a gate and keep to the left of the field ahead, going down a hill to a stile. Cross it, following the sign to **Yarningdale for Mardon**, and follow the path along the left-hand edge of the field. Go through the kissing-gate at the end, and, at the path junction after a few yards, turn right. Soon after cross a stile into a field and keep to the right, alongside a stream. Then cross a stile into a small wood. Leave the wood through a gate. Do not follow the track immediately on the right, but take the path just beyond it (signed to Yarningdale for Mardon, though the sign is somewhat obscured). Cross a stile into a green lane and climb between high banks, with the trees

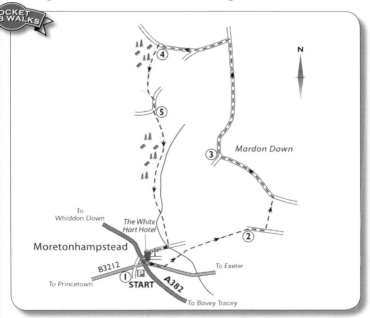

The almhouses, Moretonhampstead.

forming a tunnel overhead. At the top go through a kissing-gate onto a track (signed to the path to **Mardon Down**).

2 The track joins a surfaced lane; follow this and after 150 yards, look for a gap on the left with two gates. Take the right-hand one, which bears a sign indicating that it is the bridlepath to the moor. (Look back for a view across the farms to the open moor.) A path takes you between a hedge and a fence to a gate (with another good view to your left); on the other side of the gate is **Mardon Down**. Follow the path through the bracken to a road; turn left here and continue along the road. There is now an outstanding view to the left and ahead, taking in most of south-eastern Dartmoor.

3 At the T-junction in ½ mile, turn right (signed to **Clifford Bridge**). In ½ mile you cross a cattle grid, and 600 yards further on you will come to a junction; turn left (signed to **Chagford**). At the next junction, after 500 yards, follow the main lane round to

the right as it climbs. (At the top is an extensive view to the left.) Continue along the road as it now descends and swings to the right.

At a stile on the left, follow the public footpath sign to **Moreton**, to enter an enchanting wood. Leaving the wood, cross a stile into a green lane and turn left. You come out at a drive; turn left and immediately right into a lane, continuing to follow the footpath sign for Moreton.

After 200 yards, as the lane swings sharply right, go straight on down a track (still signed to **Moreton**). When the main track swings right to a house, go straight on, along a smaller track; when that bends right after a few yards, go straight on again, down a green lane. This descends through a wood to a gate and then continues along a particularly pretty stretch, with a stream to your left. You finally leave the wood via a gate, keeping to the bottom of the field that follows to a gate on the left. Go down some steps and then through a gate on the right. Then bear left, following the sign for **Millbrook Bridge** and **Lime Street**. Go down a field and through a gap in a bank. Continue along the bottom of the next field and bear left through a gate alongside the stream. Cross a footbridge and a stile on the left; now turn right to follow the right-hand boundary of a field. At its end, go through a gate onto a lane and turn right. This lane climbs into **Moretonhampstead**; at the junction in the centre of the town go straight across to the **White Hart**.

Places of interest nearby

About 3 miles outside Moretonhampstead, on the road to Princetown, is the **Miniature Pony Centre**, where children can ride the ponies and handle other animals.
☎ 01647 432400

The Forest Inn

This **exploration of** central Dartmoor provides a magnificent taste of the moor without strenuous effort. It takes you from the attractive hamlet of Hexworthy onto Down Ridge, where there are reminders of Dartmoor's principal industry in previous centuries, tin mining. The route is not only an interesting introduction to the industrial archaeology of the area, however; the views from the ridge are quite outstanding. The sheer scale of the area, with rolling hills stretching to the horizon in every direction and the sky a great vault above, will take your breath away.

THE PUB

The **Forest Inn** is a fairly modern pub, light and airy, and with an attractive ambience and a warm welcome. It is divided into four interconnecting rooms, two of which are furnished with comfortable armchairs and offer a range of

Distance — 3¾ miles.

OS Explorer OL28 Dartmoor. GR 655726.
Relatively easy terrain, mainly along tracks and roads.
There is one short climb at the start, and one stretch across
the open moor, but neither is too demanding.

Starting point The Forest Inn. There is no objection to
customers leaving their cars in the pub car park while they
walk, but please ask first. If you are not visiting the pub,
there is parking at the end of the road above it, and you
can start the walk at point 5.

How to get there Turn south from the B3357 between Two
Bridges and Dartmeet, following the signs for Hexworthy and
the Forest Inn.

newspapers, books and games to keep you entertained (one of
them also has a cosy open fire in winter). The two other rooms
constitute the eating area. At the back is a pleasant family room,
and there are tables outside on a sheltered patio. The food is
mainly home-made, and ranges from soup, rolls and jacket
potatoes to traditional favourites such as cottage pie and their
interesting boozy beef pie.

*Open from 11.30 am to 2.30 pm and from 6 pm to 11 pm,
Monday to Friday, and all day on Saturday and Sunday.*
☎ *01364 631211*

Follow the road which winds up the hill from the **Forest Inn**.
At the junction after about 200 yards, follow the main road to
the left. Almost immediately you will see a stile on your right,
which you cross, and then follow the track. (You immediately

get a superb view to your left, across the **Dart valley** to **Yar Tor** and **Sharp Tor**.) The track narrows to a path and then broadens again as you cross the field to a stile. Continue along the track to a further stile, which takes you onto the open moor. Soon after the track curves round to the right, you will see a cross on your left. This is one of a series that marked the **Monks' Path**, a medieval route that linked Buckfast Abbey on the eastern edge of the moor with Tavistock Abbey on the western edge. You pass a ruined building and then the track goes right to cross the interestingly named **O Brook**.

2 On the other side you have a choice.

*If you go a short distance to the left you can explore the tin-mining remains of **Hooten Wheals**. The mounds alongside the O Brook here are the spoil heaps of the earliest tinners, who panned*

The view from Deep Swincombe.

the brook for the precious ore. The deep gully on the right is a girt, formed by the tinners as they dug into the hillside in search of more tin when the stream was exhausted. Beyond it are the remains of Hooten Wheals, a more modern, industrial mine. All that can be seen now, apart from the spoil heaps, are the drying floor and the buddle, in which the ore was washed.

To continue the walk, turn right after crossing the brook. The track then takes you gently up **Down Ridge** to the **Henroost**, another mine, where you can see the remains of the shafts. It is glorious up here, with just the rolling moor, the vast sky and occasionally the bleating of sheep in the distance.

At the **Henroost**, where the track ends, bear right and follow a rough path to the **O Brook**, where you will find a shallow ford. Cross the brook (it is not very wide here, so if you do not want to use the ford you should be able to find a place to jump across). On the other side is a short track; follow that to the point where it peters out. Here there are three rough paths; take the one on the left. As you come over the brow of the hill, a superb vista opens up ahead, and you can see the scale of Dartmoor. Wherever you look – ahead, behind or to either side – there are rolling, barren contours and strange tors. Soon you will see the valley of **Deep Swincombe** coming down on your left. Make your way to it and follow it down into the valley below. Towards the bottom cross a stile and make your way to a clear track visible ahead of you.

4 Turn right when you reach it. After a short distance you cross a bridlepath; carry straight on along the main track, which swings right in 300 yards.

Soon after, you will find the remains of a medieval blowing house on the left. This was where the tinners brought their ore to be smelted. Look out for the mortar stone, on which the ore was pounded by a giant water-powered pestle to break it up, and the mould stone into which the molten tin was poured to make ingots. Just beyond the blowing house are the ruins of the **Gobbett Mine**.

Beyond them, go round a gate to a road and turn right.

5 After about 300 yards you cross a cattle grid and, a few yards further on, there is a track leading left. Follow that, cross the surfaced drive, and continue along the track as it goes down past some houses and then curves right. It becomes a surfaced lane and swings left to the **Forest Inn**.

Places of interest nearby

About 5 miles from Hexworthy, in Princetown, is the **High Moorland Visitor Centre**, which has displays, features and a video of life on Dartmoor, past and present.
☎ 01822 832093

14 Buckland Monachorum

The Drake Manor Inn

Buckland Monachorum is a delightful little village with strong associations with the Drake family – Sir Francis Drake lived at Buckland Abbey, not far away. This beautiful circuit takes you across open downland, with some marvellous views, and down to the valley of the River Tavy at its confluence with its tributary the Walkham. A particularly lovely stretch then follows, along the banks of the Walkham and through scattered mining remains. You then climb back to the bracken-covered common for breathtaking views of Dartmoor, before returning to Buckland Monachorum.

Devon

THE PUB The **Drake Manor Inn** is a low-beamed, 16th century inn. There is a snug, carpeted lounge, decorated with miniature cups, and a public bar, which displays old photographs and ships' badges; both have a wood-burning stove. The dining room has a slate floor and is furnished with pine tables and chairs. There is a beer garden outside. The menu ranges from bar snacks like baguettes and ploughman's lunches to steaks and fish.

Open from 11.30 am to 2.30 pm, Monday to Friday; from 11.30 am to 3 pm on Saturday; and from noon to 10.30 pm on Sunday.
☎ *01822 853892*

1 Turn right from the pub and follow the lane out of the village. Continue as it swings left (signed to **Coppicetown**). At the next junction go straight on and, after another 100 yards, you will see a public bridleway sign pointing to a drive on the right. Follow the drive to the left round a house. Then go right along a green lane. When you come to a gate, follow the lane to the

left, enjoying its pleasant tranquillity as it runs down to a stream. (The stream is not deep but you will get your feet wet as you cross it.) The lane then winds up the valley side and comes out at a surfaced lane.

Turn left and, at the junction in 300 yards, turn right into a lane, which climbs steadily but not too steeply for 500 yards. Go through the gate at the end and along the track, following the public bridleway sign. When the track forks, go straight on. You now get a lovely view up the valley of the **River Tavy**. Keep to the track as it descends through the bracken to the woods alongside the river. When it forks, go right, following the track as it winds left and then right. This is a pleasant stretch of woodland, with the river audible and then visible on your left. Soon after it comes into view you will see a path leading off the track to the left to a footbridge across the **River Walkham**, at its confluence with the **Tavy**. Take it and cross the bridge.

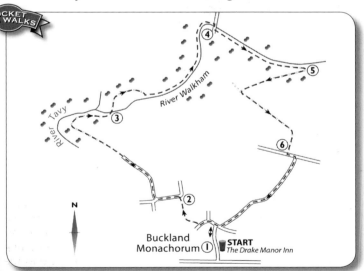

The River Tavy at its confluence with the Walkham.

3 Follow the left bank of the **Tavy** for a short distance before swinging right between two enormous rocks to reach the right bank of the **Walkham**. After a while the path broadens to a track and curves and climbs left, away from the river. It passes a house and swings left and then right, still climbing. At the junction at the top of the climb, go right. (You can still hear the river down on your right but it is no longer visible.) Past another house, the track swings right, back to the river, where it narrows again to a path and follows the river. This is a particularly attractive part of the walk, as you pass among the moss-covered trees, with the river rushing by on your right and giant rocks dominating the hillside on your left. About ¼ mile after passing the ruins of a copper mine, including the engine-house chimney, you go through a gate and follow the path to the left of a house. It comes out at a track, which you follow to a lane and turn right.

Cross a bridge and a cattle grid, and turn left to follow the other bank upstream. The river flows much more quietly here. The path becomes a track, which can be muddy after rain. After about ¾ mile it joins a track from the right.

Turn sharp right along the new track. When it turns sharply to the left, go straight on along a less clearly defined track, which swings left to cross a bridge over a disused railway line and then goes right again. It comes out onto open downland and crosses a grassy track; turn left along it. (Look to your right and behind here for a breathtaking view of the tors of western Dartmoor.) The new track runs for about ½ mile to the corner of a fence and wall. Towards the end it can become a little confusing as other tracks branch off it, but if you find a fence and wall in front of you, just turn left and you will come to the corner after a short distance. Keeping the fence on your left, go down to a car park and a road.

Turn left, and then in 250 yards turn right down a narrow lane, which runs down for almost a mile to **Buckland Monachorum**. When you come to a T-junction turn right and at the next T-junction left to return to the centre of the village and the **Drake Manor Inn**.

Places of interest nearby

Sir Francis Drake's home, **Buckland Abbey**, now owned by the National Trust, is 1 mile away.
☎ 01822 853607

Just outside the village is the **Garden House**, a beautiful themed garden.
☎ 01822 854769

15 Beesands

The Cricket Inn

Superb coastal views, quiet beaches, pretty woods, flower-filled green lanes, farm paths – this walk has them all, without too much effort to enjoy them. From the one-street fishing village of Beesands you follow the South West Coast Path north between the long beach and pretty Widdicombe Ley, before heading inland along a farm path to the delightful woodland around Widdicombe House. A green lane then takes you south to the hamlet of Beeson, where you join little-used lanes and another green lane before taking farm paths back to rejoin the Coast Path at Hallsands.

HE UB Apart from the sign, the **Cricket Inn** looks like just another of the fishermen's cottages strung out along the shore, facing the elements. Inside, however, it is warm and welcoming. There is just one room, divided into two sections: a panelled bar area with a wooden floor and a nicely furnished and carpeted dining area. Old photographs of the village decorate the walls, and an open fire welcomes visitors in winter. Outside there are tables and benches overlooking the beach. As one would expect from its situation, local fish is a particular speciality, and on the menu are superb seafood pancakes and hand-picked crab. The usual array of sandwiches and salads is on offer, as well as daily main course specials.

Open in winter from 11 am to 3 pm and from 6 pm to 11 pm, Monday to Friday; from 11 am to 11 pm on Saturday; and from noon to 11 pm on Sunday; open all day every day in summer.
☎ *01548 580215*

Distance – 4 miles.

OS Explorer OL20 South Devon. GR 819403.
Generally easy paths, green lanes and lanes, with few significant hills.

Starting point The Cricket Inn, Beesands. The pub does not have a car park, but there is parking along the sea wall just opposite it.

How to get there Turn south off the A379 Kingsbridge to Dartmouth road just west of Stokenham and follow the signs to Beesands.

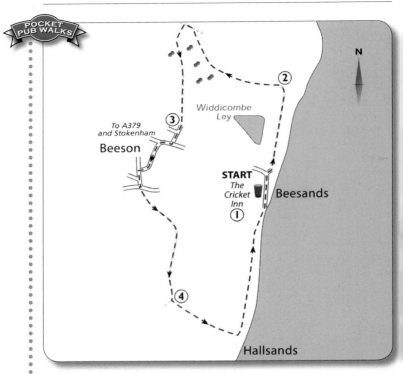

1 Turn left as you leave the pub and walk back along the road the way you came in. When it bends left, turn right, and then left along a broad surfaced track, following the Coast Path sign for **Torcross**. (You now get a good view ahead of **Start Bay**.) The track runs between **Widdicombe Ley** and the beach and you pass a football pitch. Where the track swings left to a house, follow it round.

2 Pass the house and take the path straight ahead, climbing away from the beach. At the junction in about 100 yards, turn left (signed to **Widewell**). Cross a stile into a field and keep left. Then

go over a stile on the right and cross a track before a stile takes you into a wood. The path skirts the edge of the wood and passes a house; then it joins a surfaced drive, where you go straight on, following the footpath sign. After 100 yards or so you will see a public footpath sign; turn left down the path, following the direction for **Beeson**. The path runs through the wood and then alongside a high wall, past **Widdicombe House**, to a stile. Keep to the left of the field ahead to a stile. (You now get an impressive view across the South Hams countryside, with, on a clear day, Dartmoor visible in the distance on the right.) Go through a gate and cross a track to another track, keeping a farmhouse on your right. Where the track ends, go through the gate into a green lane. When you arrive at a track, go straight on.

The track comes out onto a lane at **Beeson**. Turn right here and then go left at the T-junction. After a few yards, where the main lane swings left, turn right. A few yards further on you come to another junction; this time go left. The lane winds and climbs to

Start Point.

a T-junction; turn left again. At the next junction go straight on and, in a few yards, as the main lane goes left, go straight on along a track marked 'farm only'. As you continue to climb you get superb views across the countryside to the right and along the coast ahead to **Start Point**. When you come to a gate, turn left down a green lane and descend through a tunnel of trees to a gate. Go through the gate, turn left to skirt some buildings, and go through a gate into a green lane. This descends to a gate and continues on the other side.

6 After another 500 yards or so you will see a sign pointing left to **Hallsands**; turn off the green lane and go through a gate into a field, keeping to the left. You pass a fishing lake down on the right. At the end of the field go right, following the sign for **Beesands** via the coast and **Hallsands**. Keep to the left of the next field to a gate into a green lane. A further gate takes you into a field; keep to the right to join the **Coast Path**. (On your right is Hallsands beach, with a view round the bay to Start Point.) Turn left to follow the fence to a gate. You then cross several more fields separated by gates, keeping to the right all the time. After a while you will see the long stretch of **Beesands beach** ahead of you. At the path junction just above Beesands, go straight on, following the acorn **Coast Path** waymark. Go through a gate and down to **Beesands**, finally joining a road, which you follow to return to the pub.

Places of interest nearby

About 4 miles north of Beesands, near Torcross, is the national nature reserve of **Slapton Ley**.
☎ 01548 580466

On the other side of Kingsbridge, 8 miles from Beesands, is **Sorley Tunnel Adventure Farm**.
☎ 01548 854078